MW00694903

# This Book Belongs To

Leslie Ann

# For My Daughter

Thoughts on Love, Life, and Happiness

Ariel Books
Andrews and McMeel
Kansas City

ISBN: 0–8362–3028–0

Library of Congress Catalog Card Number: 92–73438

Marbleized endpapers © 1985
by Katherine Radcliffe

# CONTENTS

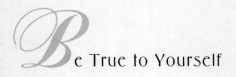

$\mathcal{B}$e True to Yourself

*For My Daughter*

No one can make you feel inferior
without your consent.

—ELEANOR ROOSEVELT

The delights of self-discovery are
always available.

—GAIL SHEEHY

One is not born a woman—one becomes one.

—SIMONE DE BEAUVOIR

Don't compromise yourself. You are all you've got.

—JANIS JOPLIN

*For My Daughter*

No one can build his security upon
the nobleness of another person.

—WILLA CATHER

10

*T*o learn to know one's self, to pursue the avenues of self-development, that's what I call creative aging.

—ADA BARNETT STOUGH

*For My Daughter*

*I*t is not easy to find happiness in ourselves, and it is impossible to find it elsewhere.

—AGNES REPPELIER

*Be True to Yourself*

Let the world know you as you are,
not as you think you should be, because
sooner or later, if you are posing, you will
forget the pose, and then where are you?

—Fanny Brice

# Follow Your Dreams

*For My Daughter*

*E*veryone has talent. What is rare is the courage to follow the talent to the dark place where it leads.

—ERICA JONG

*Y*ou can have anything you want if you want it desperately enough. You must want it with an exuberance that erupts through the skin and joins the energy that created the world.

—SHEILA GRAHAM

*For My Daughter*

*I*f you think you can, you can. And if
you think you can't, you're right.

—MARY KAY ASH

*W*e must overcome the notion that
we must be regular. It robs us of the
chance to be extraordinary and leads us to
the mediocre.

—UTA HAGEN

*S*triving for excellence motivates you. Striving for perfection is demoralizing.

—Dr. Harriet Braiker

*O*ptimism is the faith that leads to achievement. Nothing can be done without hope and confidence.

—Helen Keller

*For My Daughter*

*S*ometimes we look so intently toward
the pinnacle that we stumble over the
steps leading to it. Development begins
just where you are.

—MRS. HERMAN STANLEY

It's good to have an end to journey towards; but in the end, it is the journey itself that makes the difference.

—URSULA K. LE GUIN

Beauty

*For My Daughter*

Beauty does not come with creams and lotions. God can give us beauty, but whether that beauty remains or changes is determined by our thoughts and deeds.

—DELORES DEL RIO

Elegance does not consist in putting on a new dress.

—Coco Chanel

Beauty comes in all sizes—not just size 5.

—Roseanne Arnold

*For My Daughter*

*A*dornment is never anything but a reflection of the self.

—Coco Chanel

You can take no credit for beauty at 16. But if you are beautiful at 60, it will be your soul's own doing.

—MARIE STOPES

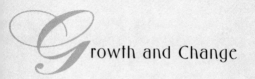

Growth and Change

*For My Daughter*

Only in growth, reform, and change,
paradoxically enough, is true security to
be found.

—ANNE MORROW LINDBERGH

*B*e bold. If you're going to make an error, make a doozy.

—BILLIE JEAN KING

*I*ndecision is fatal. It is better to make a wrong decision than to build up a habit of indecision.

—MARIE BENYON REY

*For My Daughter*

*N*othing in life is to be feared. It is only to be understood.

—MARIE CURIE

*D*on't be afraid that your life will end. Be afraid that it will never begin.

—GRACE HANSEN

You don't get to choose how you are going to die. Or when. You can only decide how you are going to live.

—JOAN BAEZ

*For My Daughter*

*E*verybody knows that if you are too careful, you are so occupied on being careful that you are sure to stumble over something.

—GERTRUDE STEIN

*Y*ou may be disappointed if you fail,
but you are doomed if you don't try.

—BEVERLY SILLS

*A*dventure is worthwhile in itself.

—AMELIA EARHART

Career

*For My Daughter*

To feel valued, to know, if only once in a while, that you can do a job well is an absolutely marvelous feeling.

—BARBARA WALTERS

*D*on't shut yourself up in a bandbox just because you are a woman, but understand what is going on, and educate yourself to take part in the world's work, for it all affects you and yours.

—LOUISA MAY ALCOTT

*For My Daughter*

Always be smarter than the people who hire you.

—LENA HORNE

*H*ow many cares one loses when one decides not to be something, but to be someone.

—COCO CHANEL

Maturing

*For My Daughter*

The secret of staying young is to live honestly, eat slowly, and lie about your age.

—LUCILLE BALL

You grow up the day you have your first real laugh—at yourself.

—ETHEL BARRYMORE

44

*Maturing*

The years a woman subtracts from her age are not lost. They are added to the ages of other women.

—DIANE DE POITIERS

*For My Daughter*

Nature gives you the face that you have at 20, but it is up to you to merit the face you have at 50.

—Coco Chanel

*W*hat is important is to keep learning, to enjoy challenge, and to tolerate ambiguity. In the end there are no certain answers.

—MARINA HORNER

*For My Daughter*

*G*rowing up is, after all, only the understanding that one's unique and incredible experience is what everyone shares.

—DORIS LESSING

*I*n youth we learn. In age we understand.

—MARIE EBNER VON ESCHENBACH

*W*e grow neither better nor worse as we get old, but more like ourselves.

—MARY LAMBERTON BECKER

# Men and Marriage

*For My Daughter*

Marriage is not just spiritual communion and passionate embraces; marriage is also three-meals-a-day and taking out the trash.

—Dr. Joyce Brothers

*P*ains do not hold a marriage together. It is threads, hundreds of tiny threads, which sew people together throughout the years.

—SIMONE SIGNORET

*N*ever trust a husband too far or a bachelor too near.

—HELEN ROWLAND

*For My Daughter*

*L*ove doesn't just sit there, like a
stone, it has to be made, like bread;
remade all the time, made new.

—URSULA K. LE GUIN

*T*rust your husband, adore your
husband, and get as much as you can in
your own name.

—ADVICE TO JOAN RIVERS
FROM HER MOTHER

*D*on't marry a man to reform him—
that's what reform schools are for.

—MAE WEST

*I*t doesn't matter what you do in the
bedroom, as long as you don't do it in the
streets and frighten the horses.

—MRS. PATRICK CAMPBELL

etting along with men isn't what's truly important. The vital knowledge is how to get along with a man. One man.

—PHYLLIS McGINLEY

*Sexiness wears thin after a while, and beauty fades, but to be married to a man who makes you laugh everyday, ah, now that's a real treat!*

—JOANNE WOODWARD

# Motherhood
## and Family

*For My Daughter*

No matter how many communes anybody invents, the family always creeps back.

—MARGARET MEAD

There is probably nothing like living together for binding people to each other.

—IVY COMPTON-BURNETT

*A* mother is not a person to lean on,
but a person to make leaning unnecessary.

—DOROTHY CANFIELD FISHER

*T*here is a lot more to being a woman
than being a mother. But there is a lot
more to being a mother than most people
suspect.

—ROSEANNE ARNOLD

*For My Daughter*

I hope I have shown you that loving means letting go, too. Letting go of needing to be loved, and simply loving. It is somewhat like the way you girls tend your plants. Their response is borne of your initial actions. Love blooms that way too. When we love, we become loved.

—ISA KOGON, TO HER DAUGHTERS

*Motherhood and Family*

*I*f we try to control and hold onto our
children, we lose them. When we let them
go, they have the option of returning to
us more fully.

—ANNE WILSON SHAEF

*For My Daughter*

Women, as the guardians of children, possess great power. They are the moulders of their children's personalities and the arbiters of their development.

—ANN OAKLEY

God knows a mother needs fortitude and courage and tolerance and flexibility and patience and firmness and nearly every other brave aspect of the human soul. But . . . I praise casualness. It seems to me the rarest of virtues. It's useful enough when children are small. It is important to the point of necessity when they are adolescents.

—PHYLLIS MCGINLEY

*For My Daughter*

*I* have always looked on child rearing not only as a work of love and duty, but as a profession that was fully as interesting and challenging as any honorable profession in the world, and one that demanded the best that I could bring to it.

—ROSE KENNEDY

Pressed for rules and verities,
All I recollect are these:
Feed a cold and starve a fever.
Argue with no true believer.
Think-too-long is never-act.
Scratch a myth and find a fact.

—PHYLLIS MCGINLEY

# Facing Adversity

*For My Daughter*

We could never learn to be brave
and patient if there were only joy in the
world.

—HELEN KELLER

The true way of softening one's
troubles is to solace those of others.

—MADAME DE MAINTENON

Laugh and the world laughs with you,
Weep and you weep alone.
For the sad old earth,
Must borrow its mirth.
But has trouble enough of its own.

—ELLA WHEELER WILCOX

*For My Daughter*

Regret is an appalling waste of energy;
you can't build on it; it's only good for
wallowing in.

—KATHERINE MANSFIELD

It is better to light a candle than to curse the darkness.

—ELEANOR ROOSEVELT

Flowers grow out of dark moments.

—CORITA KENT

# Words of Wisdom

*For My Daughter*

General notions are generally wrong.

—LADY MARY WORTLEY MONTAGU


Life is under no obligation to give us what we expect.

—MARGARET MITCHELL


76

*Words of Wisdom*

*A* little credulity helps one through life
very smoothly.

—Mrs. Gaskell

*I*f we'd only stop trying to be happy
we'd have a pretty good time.

—Edith Wharton

*For My Daughter*

If you want to catch a trout, don't go fishing in a herring barrel.

—ANN LANDERS

Till what's empty. Empty what's full. Scratch where it itches.

—ALICE ROOSEVELT LONGWORTH

*Words of Wisdom*

*K*eep breathing.

—SOPHIE TUCKER

*H*appiness is good health and a bad memory.

—INGRID BERGMAN

The text of this book was set in Fournier
with display in Florentine and Zither by
Dix Type Inc., of Syracuse, New York.

Design by Maura Fadden Rosenthal.